The Dream Scene

How to Interpret and Understand Your Dreams

Reviewed and endorsed by
Phyllis Koch-

By Alison Bell

Illustrated by Wesla Weller

•• a fresh! book ••

Lowell House
Juvenile
Los Angeles

CONTEMPORARY BOOKS
Chicago

To Alexa, who knows better than I
how to incorporate the wonder
of her dreams into her life
—A.B.

Fresh is an imprint of Lowell House Juvenile,
a division of RGA Publishing Group, Inc.

PUBLISHER: Jack Artenstein
GENERAL MANAGER, JUVENILE DIVISION: Elizabeth D. Wood
EDITORIAL DIRECTOR: Brenda Pope-Ostrow
DIRECTOR OF PUBLISHING SERVICES: Mary D. Aarons
SENIOR EDITOR: Amy Downing
COVER DESIGN: Lisa-Theresa Lenthall
INTERIOR DESIGN: Tanya Maiboroda
COVER PHOTOGRAPH: Tony Stone Images, 1994

Library of Congress Catalog Card Number: 94-32736

ISBN: 1-56565-160-X

10 9 8 7 6 5 4 3 2

Lowell House books can be purchased at special discounts
when ordered in bulk for premiums and special sales.
Contact Department VH at the following address:

Lowell House Juvenile
2029 Century Park East
Suite 3290
Los Angeles, CA 90067

Contents

Introduction: The Stuff of Dreams

By day, you're a mild-mannered sixth grader. You go to school each day, hit the books every afternoon, and don't talk back to your parents (well, most of the time).

But at night, when you're dreaming, anything and everything can happen! You fly like Peter Pan, talk to animals, travel to distant planets, and date your favorite celebrities.

So what do your dreams mean? This book is for all of you who have ever asked this question. And, considering that if you live to be seventy you'll spend up to six years of your life dreaming, it's an important question to ask!

Throughout most of history, people thought dreams were primarily messages from God (or gods) or from the devil or demons. Then later, between the 18th and 19th centuries, people thought that dreams were caused primarily by something physical, such as a stomachache or a cold.

All this changed toward the end of the 19th century, when modern psychology, the study of people's emotions and behavior, was born. During this time, dream theorists began to believe that dreams expressed people's thoughts and feelings.

Most psychologists and psychiatrists today agree that dreams can reveal new insights into our personalities. They reflect our feelings, our thoughts, our hopes, our problems. By examining your dreams, you can learn a lot about how you see yourself and the world around you.

Noted dream expert Robert Langs points out in his book *Decoding Your Dreams*, "You will find that paying attention to your dreams is very much like having a personal counselor, whose entire reason for existence is to register your perceptions, work over your conflicts, and suggest potential avenues of response.

"In point of fact, this counselor is a genius, consistently pointing out aspects of your situation and your feelings that you have overlooked or ignored or tried to keep at bay."

Of course, figuring out your dreams isn't always easy. Often dreams don't make much sense; they seem to "speak" their own language. In the following chapters, you'll learn how to "translate" your dreams and your friends' dreams, as well as how to remember more of your own dreams.

Included in the back of the book is a Dream Keeper for recording your dreams and the dreams of your friends. Throughout the book you'll also find fun exercises called Dream Keeper Schemes, to do alone or with your friends, that will help you explore your dreams even further.

In the pages ahead, I hope you'll have lots of fun and make important discoveries about yourself—and, of course, have many sweet dreams along the way!

The Sleeping and Dreaming Cycle

In a way, you're already an expert on sleeping and dreaming...after all, you do it every night! Before you start interpreting your dreams and the dreams of your friends, take a few minutes to learn about what happens every time you close your eyes and sleep.

Non-REM and REM Sleep

There are two different types of sleep: REM, or rapid-eye-movement sleep, known as "dreaming" sleep; and non-REM sleep, known as "quiet" sleep. During non-REM sleep, your body is at rest. It is capable of movement, but your brain stops sending messages to your body to move, so you usually lie still. Your heartbeat and breathing are normal. The mind is also at rest during non-REM sleep. There is very little dreaming, if any at all.

During REM sleep, your mind becomes very active. This is when you do almost all of your dreaming. Your body also becomes more active. Behind closed eyelids, your eyes dart back and forth rapidly as if you were watching a hyper-speed tennis match. Your heart rate and breathing speed up, too.

Ironically, despite this increased activity, your body is basically paralyzed during REM sleep. The most you're able to do is twitch your hands, feet, and face. The rest of your muscles are unable to move. The brain signals sent to tell your muscles to move are blocked in the spinal cord. (That's why any sleepwalking you do is done during non-REM sleep.)

This may, in part, explain that scary feeling you may have experienced in a dream when you try to

How do scientists know so much about dreaming and sleep states?

By monitoring the sleep of thousands of volunteers, researchers in countless experiments have measured sleepers' heart action, respiration, eye and body movements, and brain waves to distinguish the different stages of sleep. Part of the experiments also include waking up people while they're in a REM state and simply asking, "Were you dreaming?" Almost always, the answer is yes.

REM sleep was first discovered in 1953 by a researcher at the University of Chicago named Eugene Aserinsky. While observing sleeping babies for an experiment, he noticed that during certain times the babies' eyes moved back and forth rapidly under their closed eyelids. This led to further experiments on adults, which showed that if people were woken up during this rapid eye movement, they almost always remembered a dream.

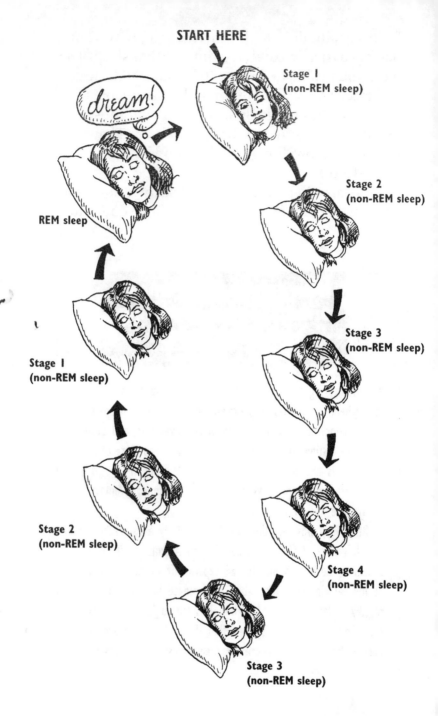

START HERE

Stage 1
(non-REM sleep)

dream!

REM sleep

Stage 2
(non-REM sleep)

Stage 1
(non-REM sleep)

Stage 3
(non-REM sleep)

Stage 2
(non-REM sleep)

Stage 4
(non-REM sleep)

Stage 3
(non-REM sleep)

8

escape from someone or something, only to find you're rooted to the spot. But maybe it's a good thing you can't move around freely while you dream. Otherwise, one night in the middle of a dream about your current crush, you might awaken to find yourself knocking at his or her front door in an effort to act out your dream!

The Sleep Cycle

Even though you don't always remember your dreams, you dream every night. Your brain is a dream machine, producing over two hours' worth of dreams during eight hours of sleep. Some research shows that most people experience anywhere from three to nine dreams a night.

When you first begin to fall asleep, you are in non-REM sleep. There are four stages to non-REM sleep: Stage 1 begins when you first feel drowsy and start to fall asleep. You then pass through stages 2, 3, and 4. Each stage puts you into a deeper and deeper sleep.

After reaching stage 4, the deepest stage of sleep, you return through stages 3 and 2 back to stage 1. You then enter REM sleep and begin dreaming.

REM sleep is a light state of sleep. But even if your sleep is disturbed—let's say the alarm clock goes off—you may not wake up easily if you're in the middle of a really interesting dream. Or, you may work the alarm clock into your dream before it finally rouses you out of your sleep.

This entire non-REM/REM cycle takes about ninety minutes and is repeated throughout the night.

Dreaming Time

During the first few non-REM/REM cycles, you don't spend much time dreaming. The first REM period may last only five or ten minutes. As the night progresses, however, you spend more and more time in REM sleep and less in non-REM sleep. By the end of the night, you may be spending as much as an hour at a time in REM sleep.

Adults spend 25 percent of their nightly sleep in the REM state. Babies spend up to 50 percent in REM sleep. (No one knows why babies need more REM sleep, but experts believe that it somehow helps with a baby's development.) Kids also spend slightly more time in REM sleep than adults. However, according to Richard Ferber, director of pediatric sleep disorders at the Children's Hospital in Boston, by the time you hit your teens, you'll settle down to 25 percent dream time.

The Importance of Dreaming

Dreams can be important tools in examining how you feel about yourself and the world. Despite all the research done on sleep and dreaming, however, no one yet knows why people have REM sleep or why they dream. But because everyone dreams every night, researchers conclude that REM sleep and dreaming serve some sort of important function in the human mind. What research has shown is that if people go without REM sleep (alcohol and some medications deprive people of REM sleep), they become irritable, anxious, and have trouble concentrating. So it appears that everyone needs REM sleep and dreams.

Now that you know the basics of dreaming and the sleep cycle, it's time to get going on your very own Dream Keeper.

Dream On!: Using the Dream Keeper

The first step toward understanding your dreams is to start a dream journal, which is why your very own Dream Keeper is provided at the back of the book, starting on page 55. This can be the place you write down your dreams, your friends' dreams, and your interpretations of the dreams.

Right now, you may not remember many (or even any!) of your past dreams. But by writing them down and making an effort to remember them, you'll start to recall more of your dreams.

Getting Started

So, when should you start writing down all of your dreams in the Dream Keeper? Right now! Here's how to organize each dream:

1. Start out each dream by filling in the date on which you had the dream.

2. Give each dream a title. This will help you if you want to refer back to a particular dream. For example, if you dream that you're flying through a sky full of stars in a spaceship, you might entitle the dream "Starry Skies."

3. Write down the dream in as much detail as possible. Include how you were feeling, how things smelled and felt, and any colors.

4. Write the details of your dream in present, not past, tense (see examples below under "Dream Details"). This keeps the dream more immediate in your mind and helps with the flow of writing. Don't worry if you can't remember an entire dream. Write it down anyway, even if it's only a small piece or fragment.

5. Don't get hung up on spelling and grammar—this isn't an English essay! You don't have to worry about any teacher with a red pen breathing down your neck. Just let your mind flow and get the dream written down before it slips away.

Once you begin writing down your dreams, try to get in the habit of doing it every morning. At first this may seem like a big effort, but the more you do it, the easier it will become. Soon it will be as much a part of your morning ritual as brushing your teeth and changing out of your pajamas.

To get you going, here are a few entries in the dream journal of eleven-year-old Gia.

• •

Date: 9/12/94

Dream Title: "Painting Nails"

Dream Details: I'm sitting in my sister's bedroom. She's painting her nails and humming. She's using a red polish. I reach over to take the polish and she disappears through the window.

How can I get in the habit of writing in my Dream Keeper?

Keep the Dream Keeper and a pen or pencil by your bed. That way, you're more likely to write down a dream right after you wake up. If you wait too long to record a dream, chances are you'll lose it forever. Most dreams fade from our minds within ten minutes of waking up. So no matter what time of night you wake up from a dream—even if it's two o'clock in the morning—get up and write it down in your Dream Keeper!

   (If you share a room with your sister or brother and can't turn on the lights to write down a dream, stash a flashlight by your bed as well.)

Date: 9/15/94
Dream Title: "Everyone's Laughing"
Dream Details: I'm back in first grade. The teacher tells me to go outside and stand alone in the playground because I've done something wrong. All the kids start laughing at me. Paulette McDougal's in the class and she's laughing the hardest of all. I go outside and play jacks until my dad comes to take me home.

Date: 9/19/94
Dream Title: "Mom's Not Mom"
Dream Details: I'm walking home from school and everything is different. Where the park used to be,

there's a huge shopping mall. There's a Target, a Toys 'R' Us, and a K mart. I walk through Target and throw some nylons in a shopping cart. I also buy a video. I don't remember which one. When I get home, the house is empty. I feel very lonely. After a while my mom comes home. She looks like Mom, but she talks like Aunt Patty. Somehow I know she really isn't my mom. I'm about to say something, but then I wake up.

• •

Ready to start writing down some of your own dreams? Tonight is a great time to begin!

Remembering Your Dreams

Even if you keep the Dream Keeper by your bed and madly scribble down every dream as soon as you wake up, you might not always remember as much as you want to. If you're having problems recalling your dreams, these tips can help kick your memory in gear and stop your dreams from doing a disappearing act.

Sleep on It

Here are a couple of things you can do before you go to bed:

▶ Write down the day's date in your Dream Keeper right before you crawl into bed. This may sound silly, but it signals your mind, "Dreams, ready or not, I'm ready for you!"

▶ Give yourself a suggestion to remember your dreams right before you fall asleep. Here's how you do it:

Make sure your body is as relaxed as possible. To do this, first tense, then relax, all the muscles in your body, muscle group by muscle group. Start with your feet. Squeeze the muscles tight, hold for ten seconds, then release them. Continue with this exercise all the way up to your neck and facial muscles.

Once your body feels as mushy as a marshmallow, tell yourself, "I will remember my dreams when I wake up in the morning." Repeat this several times, or until you fall asleep!

Hopefully, in the morning your mind will have taken your suggestion and you'll have more memories of your dreams.

When You Wake Up in the Morning

Try these handy tips to help you remember your dreams *after* you've had them:

▶ Don't move! If you wake up knowing you had a dream but it has escaped you, stay curled up in the same position you were in while sleeping. Close your eyes and drift back into a sleepy state. Sometimes this can help unearth a dream from your memory.

▶ Ask yourself how you feel. Even if you can't remember the dream, the mood of the dream may still be with you. Are you feeling sad? Happy? Peaceful? This may also help nudge the dream back into your mind.

▶ Make a mental list of all the important people in your life. Running through all the key players—your parents, brothers and sisters, friends, even your cherished goldfish, Gertrude—may help you remember who was in your dream.

▶ Even if you recall only a small chunk of a dream, write it down anyway. Sometimes the act of writing down part of a dream will trigger you to remember more of it.

▶ Put your dream on paper using pictures only. Grab a pencil, pen, water paints, or charcoal, and sketch or paint any images you remember. As you draw, you may remember more dream details.

▶ Look through magazines or books for pictures that remind you of the dream. This exercise can also help jog your memory.

WHAT A DREAM!

General George S. Patton, *who led American troops during World War II, drew up battle plans based on his dreams. His personal secretary, Joe Rosevich, recalls many a night when Patton woke him up in the middle of the night to dictate battle plans he'd seen in his dreams. One of these dreams resulted in a successful surprise attack on German troops on Christmas Day during the Battle of the Bulge in 1944.*

Sleep Sleuthing: Making Sense of Your Dreams

Some dreams are very straightforward. For example, if you're anxious about an upcoming science test and you dream that your pen runs out of ink in the middle of an important exam and you can't finish it, the dream is most likely a reflection of the anxiety you're feeling. The exam in your dream probably stands for the science test you will soon be taking.

But often the messages of dreams are more mysterious. Your first thought is, "What does that dream mean?" Dreams have their own logic, but it's almost always not the logic you use when you're awake. This is why dreams can be so confusing.

Dream Detective

To understand your dreams, you'll need to do a little detective work. And, like any good detective, that means asking a lot of questions. On the following page are six basic questions to ask yourself when you're trying to interpret the meaning of a dream.

The answers to these questions may give you clues to solve the mystery of your dream.

1. *What are the main dream images?* (A dream image is a person, place, or thing that appears in the dream.)

2. *What immediately comes to mind when you think about each of these main dream images?*

3. *Do any of the people or animals remind you of someone else—even yourself?* (Dream characters sometimes stand for people other than themselves. They may also stand for yourself or a part of your personality.)

4. *Do the places in your dream remind you of any particular place?*

5. *How were you feeling in the dream?*

6. *Are there any recent events in your life that may have influenced the dream?* (Often the events of the past few days are reflected in your dreams.)

Take your time when answering these questions and pondering your dream. Some insights may come to you in a flash, while others can take hours, even days or weeks, to realize.

To show you how these questions can help you interpret your dream, here are three dreams and how three kids used the questions to better understand them.

A Dog-gone Dream

Eleven-year-old Luke had the following dream:

• •

Date: 6/11/94
Dream Title: "Big Dog with a Basketball"
Dream Details: I'm riding to school in a school bus. Sitting next to me is a big black dog. He's

19

wearing shorts and holding a basketball in his paws. We're talking. Suddenly the dog growls. He has big teeth. He looks like he's going to bite me. But instead of biting me, he smiles. Then he opens up the basketball and takes out a big green apple and gives it to me.

• •

When asked to answer the six questions mentioned earlier, here's what Luke came up with:

Question #1. *What are the main dream images?* The school bus, the dog, the basketball, and the apple.

Question #2. *What comes to mind when you think about each of the dream images?*

- **A school bus:** traveling.
- **A dog:** scary, big, mean. Once a dog bit me when I was a kid, and now dogs make me nervous.
- **A basketball:** sports, competition. I play forward on my school's basketball team, so when I think about a basketball it makes me feel pressure to perform.
- **An apple:** healthy, nutritious, something good for you.

Question #3. *Does the animal (in this case, the dog) remind you of anyone?* The dog reminds me of my basketball coach. He's kind of "ferocious" because he yells a lot. He's very tough on us. I'm scared of him just like I'm scared of dogs.

Question #4. *Does the place (in this case, the bus) remind you of any particular place?* It reminds me of the bus our team takes to away games.

Question #5. *How were you feeling in the dream?* Scared. But then after the dog gave me the apple, I felt relieved and happy.

Question #6. *Are there any recent events in your life that may have influenced the dream?* The game we played the other night. The coach yelled at me because I missed an easy lay-up and he yanked me out of the game for a few minutes. It really upset me.

After answering these questions, it became clear to Luke that this dream was about his feelings toward his basketball coach. The dog represented his coach, who was demanding and intimidating, and often "barked" orders at Luke on the court. The dream pointed out to him just how scared he was of his coach—especially after the game in which the coach had yelled at Luke for flubbing the lay-up.

The dream also gave Luke new insights into his coach. In the dream, Luke was prepared for the worst—for the dog to bite him. Instead, the dog gave him a present, turning out to be a friend rather than an enemy. This made Luke think twice about his coach: Could it be that the coach's bark was worse than his bite? The dream seemed to tell Luke that maybe he didn't need to be so scared.

Luke also found it significant that the dog gave him an apple, "something healthy." This helped Luke realize that deep down he's grateful to the coach. Even though the coach is tough on Luke, a part of Luke is glad, because it pushes him to become a better player. In a way, the coach is "good for him."

The dream not only helped Luke understand his feelings toward his coach, it also made Luke less afraid of him and better able to cope with him.

Do animals dream?

Studies have shown that all mammals and birds have REM sleep. From this, scientists have concluded that while you're dreaming away at night, so is your dog, Daisy, and your pet hamster, Hamlet.

The Secret Garden

Here is twelve-year-old Shawna's dream:

• •

Date: 3/21/94

Dream Title: "Garden Vine"

Dream Details: I'm in a big flower garden. Vines hang down from trees. A gardener is watering the vines. They begin to grow and take over the garden. One of the vines grabs me by the wrist. I try to shake it off, but it holds on tight. It starts to creep up my arm to my neck and strangle me. I can't breathe. I beg the gardener to do something, but she won't help me. The next thing I know, I'm out of the garden. I'm standing in the sun, in a city of big white tents. Lots of kids walk past me. They're all talking together and looking excited, and I feel left out. But then a girl wearing a yellow dress walks up to me and says, "You're going to be so happy here."

• •

Here's how Shawna answered the questions:

Question #1. *What are the main images in the dream?* The garden, the vines, the gardener, the white tents, and the girl in the yellow dress.

Question #2. *What comes to mind when you think about each of the dream images?*

- **A garden:** a quiet, peaceful place; a place where not much happens.
- **A vine:** something that clings.

23

- **A gardener:** someone who makes things grow, who takes care of things.
- **Tents:** camp, camping.
- **A girl in a yellow dress:** someone who is happy, "sunny."

Question #3. *Do the people remind you of anyone?* The gardener reminds me of my mother. She has a big garden and spends a lot of time working in it. The girl in the yellow dress reminds me of myself, because I have a yellow dress I wear all the time.

Question #4. *Do the places remind you of any particular place?* The garden reminds me of my mother's garden. The tents remind me of the camp my parents are sending me to for the summer.

Question #5. *How were you feeling in the dream?* At first I felt peaceful in the garden. Then, once the vine grabbed me, I was terrified. I felt like I'd never escape. After I got out of the garden, I still felt anxious, until I talked to the girl in the yellow dress.

Question #6. *Are there any recent events in your life that may have influenced the dream?* My parents just decided that I should go to camp for two months this summer.

This exercise helped Shawna realize that her dream had to do with her mixed feelings about going to camp for the summer. Part of her wanted to go, while the other part was scared to leave home for so long. The garden, tended by her mother, represented her home. A part of her wanted to stay in the peaceful "garden" with her family. But the other part worried that if she stayed, she would end up feeling stuck all summer.

Compounding her confusion was her relationship with her mother. While her mom was wonderful and loving, she sometimes clung to Shawna too tight, just like the vine in Shawna's dream. Shawna felt she needed some space from her.

The dream also showed that underneath her confusion, Shawna knew going to camp was the right thing to do. The dream showed this by having the happy, confident part of herself (the girl in the yellow dress) reassure the anxious part of herself.

After Shawna spent time analyzing this dream, she better understood her feelings about camp and felt a lot more excited about going!

Flying High

Kari, twelve, had the following dream:

• •

Date: 8/9/94

Dream Title: "Catching Stars"

Dream Details: I'm sitting in a plane at night. Through the window I can see a billion stars. They're so close, it's like you can touch them. Everyone in the plane opens the windows and grabs the stars. I'm so excited, I can't wait to open my window and take a star. I open the window and stick out my hand. A star hits my hand, but it's too hot and I can't hold on. I lose the star. The next thing I know, my sister's sitting next to me. We're sitting on the ground. The plane has landed.

• •

Here's how Kari answered the questions:

Question #1. *What are the main images in the dream?* The plane, stars, and my sister.

Question #2. *What comes to mind when you think about the dream images?*
- **A plane:** flying high, excitement, travel.
- **Stars:** dreaming, reaching your goals, reaching for the stars.
- **My sister:** someone who sticks by me, a friend.

Question #3. *Do the people remind you of anyone?* No. My sister is my sister.

Question #4. *Do the places in your dream remind you of any particular places?* The plane reminds me of sitting in a theater, because the seats are so narrow and you're crammed in tightly just like you are when you're sitting in the middle of a row.

Question #5. *How were you feeling in the dream?* Disappointed and frustrated. I wanted to touch the stars, but couldn't. Then the plane landed and my chance to touch the stars was over.

Question #6. *Are there any recent events in your life that may have influenced the dream?* Lately I've been feeling really disappointed and frustrated because I tried out for the school play, *Guys and Dolls*, and didn't make it.

Once Kari went through this exercise, it became clear to her that this dream represented her disappointment in not getting a part in *Guys and Dolls*. Even though she had tried to "reach for the stars" and grab her dream of becoming an actress, she had failed. The stars remained out of her reach, and her dreams were "grounded."

What was her sister doing in her dream? Her sister had also tried out for the play and had not gotten a part either. The dream pointed out how much Kari identified with her sister.

DREAM KEEPER SCHEME

Grab a friend and each select a dream from your Dream Keeper to interpret. (If your friend doesn't have a Dream Keeper, he or she can jot down a recent dream or use one of yours.) Ask your friend the six key questions and write down his or her answers. Then switch places and have your friend ask you the six key questions and write down your answers. When you're done, trade theories on what you think the dreams mean.

Universal Sleep Symbols

You have a dream that you're walking down a long road. In your hand, you're clutching an old, battered suitcase, packed with all of your most cherished possessions (including your signed photo of the cast of "Beverly Hills 90210").

Your best friend has a similar dream of walking down a road with a suitcase. Do these images in the dream—the road, the suitcase—mean the same thing in your dream as they mean in your pal's dream?

In part, maybe. Carl Gustav Jung was the first dream theorist to introduce the idea that dream images may stand for the same things in everybody's dreams. Today, many dream experts believe this to be true to a certain extent. For example, one dream expert, Tony Crisp, examined thousands of dreams over twenty-two years and, in 1990, drew up his own book of meanings for popular dream images in *Dream Dictionary*. He found that images in one person's dreams often mean the same as in the next person's. These images and their meanings make up his dictionary. (He also emphasized, however, the need for people to examine dreams for their own personal meanings as well.)

If you were to go to your local bookstore and look in the "Dreams" section, you'd find many dream dictionaries. Most of the experts who write these books have come up with the same meanings for certain dream images. For example, in most dream dictionaries, you'll find that a road in your dream generally stands for your journey through life.

Below is a mini dream dictionary of common dream images and what they may mean, compiled from several other dream dictionaries. Have fun with this dictionary! It's meant only to add to the understanding of your dreams, not to be your single guide. While you are interpreting the objects in your dreams, you should not place too much importance on any one object. Instead, try to look at your dream in general and how the objects relate to each other.

The Mini Dream Dictionary

Accident: If an accident happens to you, it may mean you wish to punish yourself for something you've done. If an accident happens to someone else, it may mean you secretly want something bad to happen to that person.

Airplane:
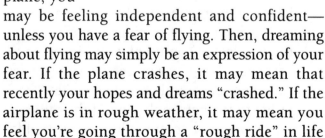
If you're traveling on an airplane, you may be feeling independent and confident—unless you have a fear of flying. Then, dreaming about flying may simply be an expression of your fear. If the plane crashes, it may mean that recently your hopes and dreams "crashed." If the airplane is in rough weather, it may mean you feel you're going through a "rough ride" in life right now.

Balcony: If you're on a balcony, you may be feeling like you're being held back from achieving your goals or dreams.

Birds: In general, birds represent freedom and self-expression. If you dream about a bird's nest, the nest may stand for your home. If you dream about birds leaving the nest, it may mean you're ready for more independence.

Boat: Any type of boat usually represents your journey through the "sea" of life. If the sea is stormy, you may be facing some problems right now. If the sea is calm, you may be feeling that you're on a smooth ride through life.

Bridge: You're "crossing" from one stage of life to another. If you dream about a fallen bridge, it may represent a lost opportunity.

Car: A car may represent whatever is the "driving" factor or energy in your life. This might be to be successful, rich, or popular. If you're driving the car, you feel in control of your life, or "in the driver's seat." If you're a passenger, you may feel as if you're not in control or that you take a "backseat" in life to the person driving. If the car crashes, it may represent a recent failure or a fear of failure.

Cemetery: Often this represents something buried in your life. For example, you may have buried feelings toward an old friend you thought you had forgotten about.

City: A city often stands for your relationship with the outside world. A city therefore might represent your school, church or synagogue, outside club, or sports team.

Digging: This may mean you're trying to uncover a truth in your life, or that you're working hard to "dig in" and solve a problem.

Diving: You may be taking a chance in your life; you're "diving" headlong into a new adventure or situation (such as trying out for a school play for the first time).

Falling: It may mean you've lost confidence or feel helpless about something. Or, it can mean you've "fallen below" your expectations or those of other people, such as your teachers.

Father: If you dream about your dad, he may be representing another authority figure in your life.

Fence: A fence in your dream often means you're facing a barrier in your life or feeling closed in. For example, maybe your parents aren't giving you the freedom you crave.

Fire: This dream image usually stands for passion, anger, or any other strong emotion that can burn out of control.

Flying: Dreams in which you're flying can mean that you aren't worried about what others think—you "fly" in the face of convention! It can also mean you feel confident about a recent accomplishment or that you feel "above" others in your life.

Garden: When a garden plays a role in your dream, it may stand for your inner self. For example, a garden overtaken with weeds may mean you feel you have some bad habits you need to work on.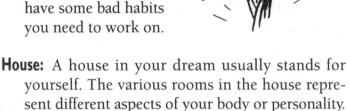

House: A house in your dream usually stands for yourself. The various rooms in the house represent different aspects of your body or personality.

Insects: If you dream that insects are attacking you, it may mean you're feeling "bugged" by nagging problems. If you are surrounded by insects, it may mean you're feeling small and insignificant, like an ant.

Mask: A mask in your dream often represents your outer self, the self you show to the world.

Moon: The image, whether it's a crescent or a full moon, often represents love and romance.

Mother: When you dream about your mom, it may represent someone who nurtures you in your life or the nurturing side of yourself.

Mountains: They often stand for the challenges you face in life.

Nude: If you dream about being nude, it may mean you feel exposed. For example, maybe you told a good pal more than you wish you had about the crush you have on your art teacher. It can also indicate that you're feeling embarrassed or ashamed about your recent behavior.

Packing: If you're all packed and ready to go, you feel ready to meet life's challenges and changes. If you can't decide what to take with you, it may mean you're undecided about what step to take next in life.

Pimples: These can stand for any personality flaws you feel you have.

Rain: When rain appears in your dream, it often stands for emotions. These can either be your emotions or those of other people you feel are "raining" on you.

Road: This often represents your direction in life. For example, if the road is straight, you may feel you're making progress. If it's winding or a dead end, you may feel you're not going anywhere.

Running: If you find yourself running in a dream, you may be trying to escape responsibilities, such as studying for an intense biology exam. It can also mean you're running away from painful feelings you don't want to face.

Siblings: Often when you dream about a brother or a sister, the person really stands for an aspect of yourself.

Storm: This often represents a burst of emotion you're feeling right now in your life.

Suitcase: A suitcase in your dream sometimes represents your innermost feelings and thoughts that you carry around inside of you.

Sun: When the sun figures prominently in your dream, it often stands for energy, life, and vitality.

Swimming: Swimming often represents confidence in yourself and your ability to "swim," not "sink," in life.

WHAT A DREAM!

Harriet Tubman *was an escaped slave who lived during the American Civil War, when slavery was widespread in the South. Before the Civil War started in 1861, she led hundreds of other slaves to safety and freedom through an "underground railroad." This railroad was a series of "safe" stops at which the slaves could meet and rest on their way to the northern United States, where slavery was not in practice.*

Tubman made nineteen rescue trips to help transport slaves from the South to the North. Despite slave-hunting patrols who were on the lookout for her, she never lost a single person she was helping to safety.

How did she do it? She claims that her dreams helped her find the safe passageways!

Teeth falling out: This can mean you're afraid of growing up and gaining new responsibilities. It can also mean you're feeling embarrassed about something.

Voyage: If you dream about going on a trip or somewhere new, you may be undertaking a new project, goal, or direction in life.

War: This may represent an inner conflict. For example, maybe you're at war with yourself about whether or not to stay in a crowd at school that's moving too fast for you.

Colors Count, Too!

Some dream experts believe that the colors in your dreams have common meanings. So the next time you're seeing red (or green or yellow) in a dream, check to see if any of these meanings apply:

Black: If something is black in your dream, it may represent something dangerous or something unknown or hidden.

Blue: If you have a dream in which blue is a common color, it can mean that you're feeling sad. Blue can also signify openness.

Brown: Brown usually represents the earth.

Green: When images in your dream are green, you may feel that it's time to make a positive change in your life—the green light for moving is on! Depending on which dream images are green, this color can also stand for jealousy or envy, as well as health, growth, and healing.

Red: Anything red in your dream is usually to be avoided. It means danger; proceed with caution!

White: This color usually stands for peace, purity, and cleanliness.

Yellow: Often this color is associated with happiness and intellect. However, it can also stand for cowardice, depending on which images in your dream are yellow.

DREAM KEEPER SCHEME

Take one of your most recent dreams and ask your friends if they've had any similar ones. Once you find a common dream you and a pal have shared (for example, let's say you both recently dreamt you were flying), use the mini dream dictionary and write down what you think the dream means, then ask your friend to do the same with his or her dream. When you're through, compare dreams. See if you interpreted them the same way or completely differently.

Things that Go Bump in the Night: Nightmares

You're running down a dark alley. A horrible creature that looks like a giant version of something you'd grow in a science experiment is chasing you.

You can hear its breathing, hear its footsteps getting closer, closer. You try to run faster, but your legs won't work. You manage to stumble a few steps when you realize you're in a blind alley. There's no way out, and the terrible thing is about to grab you....

Almost everyone has experienced a dream similar to this one.

You wake up trembling, breathing hard, and scared out of your wits. Slowly you realize with relief that it's only a dream. There's no monster in your room—just you and your little sister (even though she can be a monster herself sometimes).

Nightmares are scary not only because of how you feel during your dream, but how they make you feel afterward. It can take hours to shake off a scary dream. And sometimes a dream can haunt you the whole next day.

What Causes Nightmares?

For centuries, it was thought that nightmares were evil spirits that invaded your soul while you slept.

In the early 19th century, scary dreams were thought to be caused by what you ate. Either you ate too much, too little, or the wrong thing. It was also believed that if you slept in the wrong position, your lungs would get cramped and not allow enough air to get to your brain. The result? A terrible nightmare.

Then, in the late 19th century, dream theorists such as Sigmund Freud began investigating the link between dreams and people's inner state of mind. In part because of the research of Freud and his colleagues, today it is generally accepted that nightmares are an expression of any anxiety or fear people have. If the fear or anxiety is long-term, it may show up in the form of a recurring nightmare. For example, if you're scared of heights because you fell from a bridge when you were little, you may be haunted by a recurring nightmare of falling from a high place.

Getting Rid of Nightmares

While it can be scary to think about your nightmares, most dream experts believe interpreting a nightmare is the best way to rid yourself of it. The idea is that once you deal with the anxiety or fear in your waking life, there will be no reason to deal with it in your dreams!

For example, eleven-year-old Kyle had a recurring dream that his mother would leave him all alone in a dark, scary house. When Kyle studied his dream, he realized that it had to do with how he'd been feeling ever since his mother had remarried.

Before his stepfather came into their lives, it had always been just Kyle and his mom. Kyle's father had died when he was two years old, and his mother had raised him alone. Now that his mother had

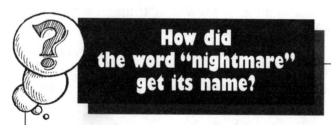

How did the word "nightmare" get its name?

The word *nightmare* comes from two words: *night* and *mare*. In ancient times, "night" had several meanings, including sleep. "Mare" comes from the word *mara*, which means to crush.

How does the verb *crush* fit in with the meaning of a nightmare?

For centuries, people believed that a nightmare was caused by a demon known as the incubus, who crushed your chest by sitting on you.

someone in her life besides Kyle, Kyle felt alone and abandoned, just as he did in the dream.

The dream prompted Kyle to talk to his mother and tell her how he was feeling. She quickly reassured him that she loved him as much as ever and nothing would ever change that. She also promised to start making a special effort to spend more one-on-one time with Kyle, as they used to before she remarried. Kyle immediately felt better. After talking to his mom, Kyle never had the dream again.

To better understand a nightmare, the next time you have a scary dream ask yourself the six key questions you learned about in chapter 3, on page 19.

Common Nightmares

Take a look at the following common nightmares and what they mean according to some dream experts who have developed their own dream dictionaries. While these meanings may shed new light on a nightmare, keep in mind that you'll learn more about a nightmare by figuring out what each dream image means to you personally.

A nightmare where you're rooted to the spot and can't move, even if something is after you:

▶ You feel "paralyzed" to move on a certain decision in your life because you're too scared to change. For example, maybe you want to try out for cheerleader or for a sports team, but you're too afraid of not making it to actually try.

▶ You're feeling stuck in a certain situation. (Maybe you hate a certain class, or you're caught in the middle of a sticky friendship dilemma.)

A nightmare where you're being followed or attacked:

▸ You're feeling like a victim. (For instance, your older sibling is constantly picking on you).

▸ You're feeling as if your emotions are out of control. (The other day, in the space of fifteen minutes, you yelled at your mom, dad, little sister, *and* your dog.) The attacker in your dream might be that part of yourself (your temper, for example) that you don't want to think about but keeps "grabbing" your attention.

A nightmare where someone you love dies:

▸ You're not as close to the person as you once were. The relationship is "dying."

▸ A part of you wants that person out of your life. For example, maybe sometimes you get so mad at your brother you wish he'd go live with another family. This feeling might show up in your dream as someone killing your brother.

A nightmare about missing an important train, plane, or bus:

▸ You are feeling as if you're not making enough progress in life or on a project you're working on. The train, plane, or bus stands for your journey through life.

A nightmare about a natural disaster such as a flood, hurricane, or earthquake:

▶ You're feeling overwhelmed by something— perhaps a test or a situation at school.

▶ Your life is going through an unusually huge change—maybe your parents are getting a divorce or you're moving.

A nightmare about a ferocious animal chasing or hurting you:

▶ You're running away from a big problem that you really should deal with. For example, you're hanging out with the wrong crowd and you know it. The animal stands for the problem.

A nightmare about the world coming to an end:

▶ You're upset because a part of your world is ending for you. For example, maybe you're unhappy about the school year being over, or about growing away from a good friend or a group of friends.

A nightmare where you die:

▶ You're going through a change that all kids experience, either physical or emotional. For example, maybe you've recently switched a circle of friends at school, because you've outgrown their interests.

43

A nightmare about taking an examination and flubbing up somehow—you arrive late, you can't find a chair, you don't have a pen:

▶ You're afraid of failing at something (not necessarily a test—it could be anything).

A nightmare about drowning:

▶ You're feeling a lot of confusing or painful emotions. They're so intense that you feel as if you're "drowning" in them.

Nightmares About Impending Disaster

You dream that someone is about to bomb your school. You try to warn your classmates over the loudspeaker, but the microphone goes dead in your hand. If you don't do something quick, your entire school will be destroyed!

As you stand there, paralyzed with fear, the clock on the wall ticks on, bringing your school closer to destruction with each passing minute....

If you had this dream on a Monday, does it mean that your school's going to get blown away on a Tuesday? Most likely, no!

While dreams that warn of some impending disaster are very upsetting, usually they have more to do with how you're feeling than with telling the future. (Maybe you'd secretly like your school to get destroyed somehow so you wouldn't have to suffer through algebra class!)

Of course, some people swear they have the ability to predict the future in a dream. And throughout history there have been some noteworthy, so-called psychic dreams.

One of the most famous examples is a dream Abraham Lincoln had a few days before he was assassinated.

He dreamt that a body was lying in the White House, surrounded by a group of weeping people. When he asked who had died, a soldier answered him, "The President. He was killed by an assassin."

Does this dream prove that Lincoln was able to tell his own future? Or was it a reflection of the fear and apprehension he felt toward his enemies? No one will ever know for sure.

Another example involves the famous sinking of the ship *Titanic* on the night of April 14, 1912. This was one of the worst sea tragedies ever, in which more than 1,500 people were killed when the ship ran into an iceberg on a trip from England to New York. On the night the ship went down, several people reported having dreamt of the accident.

In her book *Nightmare*, Sandra Shulman relates the story of one teenage girl whose uncle was a

The Senoi Indians and Nightmares

The Senoi are aboriginals who live in the jungles of Malaysia. From early childhood, Senoi children are encouraged to talk about and analyze their dreams. Every morning at breakfast, each family member relates a dream. There is even a village council where the Senoi go to discuss their dreams and try to learn from them.

In the Senoi culture, when a child has a nightmare the parents work with the child to determine what might have caused it. The parents will try to reassure the child as much as possible. For example, if a girl dreams that her parents are being mean to her and nice to her brother, they'll pick up on the feelings expressed in the dream. They'll reassure their daughter that they didn't crew member and died in the accident. Two nights before the *Titanic* sunk, the girl dreamt of walking along a local road and suddenly seeing a large ship begin to sink at one end. She heard a scream, then woke up in a panic. When she went back to sleep, she had the same horrifying—and ultimately true—dream.

mean to neglect her and will try hard not to do it again.

The Senoi are also reported to be able to influence the outcome of their dreams. At a very young age, children are taught a technique whereby they can "re-enter" a scary dream and change it into a happy one. They're also taught how to face an attacker in a dream and instead become the one who is on the attack. As a result, by the time Senoi children reach their teens, they no longer have nightmares.

This may sound farfetched, but the Senoi and their "dream culture" are well documented, despite the fact that their practices are questioned by some skeptical dream researchers. Moreover, some dream experts believe that if all of us were taught to pay that much attention to the importance of dreams, everyone could learn how to beat scary dreams for good!

DREAM KEEPER SCHEME

Want to know how to make those terrifying dreams go away for good? Jill Morris, in her book *The Dream Workbook*, suggests rewriting the dream from the scary character's point of view. This helps you understand the frightening character, which makes your dream a lot less creepy.

For example, ten-year-old Jackson had the following dream:

> *"I'm walking up the driveway to my house when the big elm tree outside turns into a person. The trunk becomes this really scary face. The branches turn into arms and won't let me go. I'm so scared and I keep screaming, but no one comes to help me."*

Afterward, Jackson was so shaken by his dream, he was scared to even walk by the tree.

When he rewrote his dream from the perspective of the tree, here's what he came up with:

> *"It's another boring day. I'm standing there all alone like always. Then the little boy who lives in the house comes walking by. I'm lonely because no one ever talks to me and I can't go anywhere, so I grab him. I feel*

sorry for him because I know he wants me to let go, but I want the company. I try to talk to him and tell him that I'm not going to hurt him, but I can't talk."

After Jackson wrote down the new version of his dream, he felt a lot less afraid. By looking at the dream from the tree's point of view, he was able to reassure himself that the tree really wasn't that scary.

Try this exercise with one of the nightmares you've written down in the Dream Keeper. You may be amazed at what you come up with and how much better it can make you feel.

Sleep Solutions: Getting Inspiration from Your Dreams

Would you like to write a poem or a short story, but don't know what to write about? Is the answer to that pesky math problem still escaping you?

If you pay enough attention, your dreams can help you become more creative and solve problems you've been wrestling with.

Throughout history, dreams have been the sources of inspiration. For example, many writers have had ideas, even entire works, come to them in dreams.

An English author named Samuel Taylor Coleridge, who lived from 1772 to 1834, wrote one of his most famous poems, "Kubla Khan," based on images that came to him in a dream. Supposedly, the author was dreaming and had dreamt all but the last verse of the poem when his housekeeper barged into his room to see if he wanted tea. He woke up and frantically scribbled down the poem— all except the missing last verse.

The writer Robert Louis Stevenson, author of such classic books as *Treasure Island* and *Dr. Jekyll and Mr. Hyde*, trained himself to remember his dreams. They often provided him with plots and ideas for his writing. One night he was struggling to come up with a plot when he dreamt of a doctor who turned into a criminal. From this dream fragment, Stevenson went on to write *Dr. Jekyll and Mr. Hyde*, which is about a well-respected doctor who was also a murderer.

Philosophers have been struck with brilliant ideas in dreams. So have artists, composers, scientists, and inventors.

The inventor of the sewing machine, Elias Howe, had an important answer come to him in a nightmare. He'd been working on the sewing machine for years, but couldn't figure out where to put the eye in the sewing-machine needle.

One night he had a nightmare where savages captured him and threatened to kill him if he didn't finish his invention. As he stared in horror at their spears, he noticed eye-shaped holes near the tips. He then realized that he'd discovered the answer to his dilemma: He should put the eye near the tip of the needle. When he woke up, he took this idea and finally finished the sewing machine!

Athletes also have sought answers in their dreams. Golfer Jack Nicklaus once improved his golf game by using a new grip that came to him while he was sleeping. According to an interview in the *San Francisco Chronicle* in 1964, Nicklaus had fallen into a bad slump—until he dreamt that he was holding his golf club differently and swinging the club perfectly. When he went to the golf course the next day, he tried out the grip he'd seen in his dream, and it worked! After the dream, Nicklaus snapped out of his golf-game slump.

WHAT A DREAM!

In 1919, a dream by leader **Mohandas Gandhi** *eventually helped his country, India, break free from England.*

India had been under harsh British rule since the late 1700s. England had just imposed a new law to suppress any activities that would help the Indians liberate themselves from the British. Gandhi was determined to help his people fight back against British rule, and for weeks meditated on how it could be done without anyone being hurt. In his autobiography, he tells how he finally had a dream suggesting that the people of India stop their normal daily routines for twenty-four hours and devote that time to prayer and fasting. The resulting nonviolent mass strikes of 1919 helped India win its eventual liberation from England in 1945.

Using Dreams to Help You

A problem doesn't have to be huge to be solved in a dream. Dreams can provide answers for small, day-to-day issues as well.

For example, let's say you're assigned to write an essay for English class on anything you want. Your mind has pulled a blank, and you're at a loss as to what topic to choose.

That night, you have a vivid dream about your dad, who is a fireman, rescuing a family from a burning building. Your father runs out of the building, carrying two children and a dog. He's a hero!

52

You wake up feeling proud of your dad.

This dream gets your creative juices flowing. What about an essay on what it's like to have a dad who's a fireman? You could write about how tough it is when he's out fighting a fire, but also how proud you are of him for being in a profession in which he helps so many people.

Voilà! A perfect essay topic.

How can you tap into any solutions your dreams may be sending you? Consistently write down your dreams and think about their meanings, and see if they may provide any answers to problems you're trying to solve.

DREAM KEEPER SCHEME

Choose a dream you've written down that particularly interests you. Write a poem or a short story based on the dream. You may surprise yourself with how good it is! Or, if you can draw, select a dream and draw a sketch or paint a picture based on the dream. You may not only learn more about the dream, but discover you've got some artistic talents to boot!

Afterword

Now that you've started writing down and interpreting your dreams, hopefully you'll keep it up throughout your life. Getting in touch with your dreams is a fun way to get to know yourself and your friends better—no matter how old you are and who your friends are.

For now, continue to stash the Dream Keeper by your side at night. Already some of its pages should be full, while others remain blank, awaiting more of your dreams. So keep dreaming and write on!

The DREAM KEEPER

This is the place to write down your dreams and your thoughts about your dreams. You don't have to show them to anybody, or you can share them with your family and friends.

Throughout this section you will find famous quotes on dreams, additional Dream Keeper Schemes, and plenty of space for you to fill in yourself! So, grab your favorite pen or pencil, sit down...and dream on!

DATE: _____

DREAM TITLE: _____

DREAM DETAILS: _____

_____

_____

_____

_____

WHAT I LEARNED FROM THIS DREAM: _____

_____

_____

_____

_____

_____

"*Wake up, Alice dear!*" *said her sister. "Why, what a long sleep you've had!*"

"*Oh, I've had such a curious dream!*" *said Alice. And she told her sister, as well as she could remember them, all these strange Adventures of hers…and when she had finished, her sister kissed her, and said, "It was a curious dream, dear, certainly; but now run in to your tea: it's getting late." So Alice got up and ran off, thinking while she ran, as well she might, what a wonderful dream it had been.*

Alice's Adventures in Wonderland,
Lewis Carroll (1832-1898)

DATE: _____

DREAM TITLE: _____

DREAM DETAILS: _____

_____

_____

_____

_____

_____

_____

_____

WHAT I LEARNED FROM THIS DREAM: _____

_____

_____

_____

_____

_____

_____

_____

DATE: _____

DREAM TITLE: _____

DREAM DETAILS: _____

_____

_____

_____

_____

_____

_____

_____

_____

WHAT I LEARNED FROM THIS DREAM: _____

_____

_____

_____

_____

_____

_____

_____

DATE: _____

DREAM TITLE: _____

DREAM DETAILS: _____

_____

_____

_____

_____

_____

_____

_____

WHAT I LEARNED FROM THIS DREAM: _____

_____

_____

_____

_____

_____

_____

_____

To sleep!
perchance to dream...

Hamlet,
William Shakespeare
(1564–1616)

59

DATE: _____

DREAM TITLE: _____

DREAM DETAILS: _____

_____

_____

Now blessings light on him
that first invented this same
sleep! It covers a man all over,
thoughts and all, like a cloak.

Don Quixote,
Miguel de Cervantes
(1547–1616)

• • • • • • • • • • • • • • • • • • •

_____

_____

_____

_____

_____

WHAT I LEARNED FROM THIS DREAM: _____

_____

_____

_____

_____

_____

_____

_____

DATE: _____

DREAM TITLE: _____

DREAM DETAILS: _____

_____

_____

_____

_____

_____

WHAT I LEARNED FROM THIS DREAM: _____

_____

_____

_____

5

DREAM KEEPER SCHEME

In her book *Nightmare*, Sandra Shulman reports that some psychologists have had success helping kids beat nightmares by having the children tell their nightmares to stay away before they go to sleep. To give this exercise a try, sit or lie on your bed right before going to sleep. Relax and close your eyes and repeat several times: "Nightmares, go away! I won't see you tonight!"

DATE: _____

DREAM TITLE: _____

DREAM DETAILS: _____

_____

_____

_____

_____

_____

_____

_____

WHAT I LEARNED FROM THIS DREAM: _____

_____

_____

_____

_____

_____

_____

_____

_____

DATE: _____

DREAM TITLE: _____

DREAM DETAILS: _____

_____

_____

_____

_____

_____

_____

_____

WHAT I LEARNED FROM THIS DREAM: _____

_____

_____

_____

_____

_____

_____

_____

I can never decide whether my dreams are the result of my thoughts or my thoughts the result of my dreams.

D.H. Lawrence, English author (1885-1930)

● ● ● ● ● ● ● ● ● ● ● ● ● ● ● ● ● ●

DATE: _____

DREAM TITLE: _____

DREAM DETAILS: _____

_____

_____

_____

_____

_____

_____

WHAT I LEARNED FROM THIS DREAM: _____

_____

_____

_____

_____

_____

_____

_____

_____

*In dreams we catch glimpses of
a life larger than our own....
Thoughts are imparted to us far
above our ordinary thinking.*

Helen Keller,
blind-deaf author and educator
(1880-1968)

64

DATE: _____

DREAM TITLE: _____

DREAM DETAILS: _____

_____

_____

_____

_____

_____

_____

_____

_____

WHAT I LEARNED FROM THIS DREAM: _____

_____

_____

_____

_____

_____

_____

_____

_____

Dream Keeper

DATE: _____

DREAM TITLE: _____

DREAM DETAILS: _____

_____

_____

_____

_____

_____

_____

_____

_____

WHAT I LEARNED FROM THIS DREAM: _____

_____

_____

_____

_____

_____

_____

_____

_____

DATE: _____

DREAM TITLE: _____

DREAM DETAILS: _____

_____

_____

_____

_____

_____

_____

_____

WHAT I LEARNED FROM THIS DREAM: _____

_____

_____

_____

_____

_____

_____

_____

Dreams are
the touchstones of
our characters.

Henry David Thoreau,
American author and
philosopher (1817-1862)

● ● ● ● ● ● ● ● ● ● ● ● ● ● ●

67

DATE: _____

DREAM TITLE: _____

DREAM DETAILS: _____

_____

_____

_____

_____

_____

_____

_____

_____

WHAT I LEARNED FROM THIS DREAM: _____

_____

We never stop seeing,
perhaps this is why we dream.

Johann Wolfgang von Goethe,
German author (1749-1832)

_____

_____

_____

_____

DATE: _____

DREAM TITLE: _____

DREAM DETAILS: _____

_____

_____

_____

_____

_____

_____

_____

WHAT I LEARNED FROM THIS DREAM: _____

_____

_____

_____

_____

_____

_____

_____

DATE: _____

DREAM TITLE: _____

DREAM DETAILS: _____

_____

_____

_____

_____

WHAT I LEARNED FROM THIS DREAM: _____

_____

_____

_____

_____

_____

DREAM KEEPER SCHEME

Sometimes dreams relate to each other. You
may have a series of dreams about the same
person or the same place. Look back over
your recorded dreams and see if the same
people or places keep cropping up. Jot them
down, and see if looking at your dreams in a
series helps you make sense of them.

DATE: _____

DREAM TITLE: _____

DREAM DETAILS: _____

_____

_____

_____

_____

_____

_____

Dreams are true while they last, and do we not live in dreams?

Alfred Lord Tennyson,
English author (1809-1892)

_____

WHAT I LEARNED FROM THIS DREAM: _____

_____

_____

_____

_____

_____

_____

_____

71

DATE: _____

DREAM TITLE: _____

DREAM DETAILS: _____

_____

_____

_____

_____

_____

_____

_____

WHAT I LEARNED FROM THIS DREAM: _____

_____

_____

_____

_____

_____

_____

Dreams are, by definition,
cursed with short life spans.

Candace Bergen, actress

● ● ● ● ● ● ● ● ● ● ● ● ● ● ● ● ● ●

_____

72

DATE: _____

DREAM TITLE: _____

DREAM DETAILS: _____

_____

_____

_____

_____

_____

_____

_____

WHAT I LEARNED FROM THIS DREAM: _____

_____

_____

_____

_____

_____

_____

_____

DATE: _____

DREAM TITLE: _____

DREAM DETAILS: _____

_____

_____

_____

_____

_____

_____

_____

WHAT I LEARNED FROM THIS DREAM: _____

_____

_____

_____

_____

_____

_____

_____

I've dreamt in my life dreams that have stayed with me ever after, and changed my ideas; they've gone through and through me, like wine through water, and altered the color of my mind.

Emily Brontë,
British author (1818-1848)

DATE: _____

DREAM TITLE: _____

DREAM DETAILS: _____

_____

_____

_____

_____

_____

_____

_____

WHAT I LEARNED FROM THIS DREAM: _____

_____

_____

_____

_____

_____

_____

_____

_____

_____

DATE: _____

DREAM TITLE: _____

DREAM DETAILS: _____

_____

_____

_____

_____

_____

_____

_____

WHAT I LEARNED FROM THIS DREAM: _____

_____

_____

_____

_____

_____

_____

_____

_____

DREAM KEEPER NOTES

_____

_____

_____

_____

_____

_____

_____

_____

_____

_____

_____

_____

_____

_____

_____

_____

_____

_____

_____

Dreams have only one owner at a time. That's why dreamers are lonely.

Erma Bombeck,
American humorist

• • • • • • • • • • • • • • • • • • • •

77

DREAM KEEPER NOTES

_____

_____

_____

_____

_____

_____

_____

_____

_____

_____

_____

_____

_____

_____

_____

_____

_____

_____

DREAM KEEPER NOTES

_____

_____

_____

_____

_____

_____

_____

_____

_____

_____

_____

_____

_____

_____

_____

_____

_____

_____

_____

_____

Dream Keeper

DREAM KEEPER NOTES

To believe one's dreams is to spend all of one's life dreaming.
Chinese proverb